I
AM
Divine Inspirations

LATONYA MORRISON

I Am: Divine Inspirations

Copyright © 2024 by LaTonya Morrison

Printed in the United States of America First Printing, 2024

ISBN: 979-8-9892300-5-1

Leftwich Press, Inc.
Brooklyn, NY
www.LeftwichPressChristianPublishing.com

DEDICATION

I dedicate this book to God, who is the head of my life.

And to my family, I pray that one day they will read this book and want God to be a part of their lives.

TABLE OF CONTENTS

INTRODUCTION

God allowed me to write this book, so the world knows He is still our living God. God is still performing miracles, signs, and wonders. God is still talking and spreading His word through regular people like me. God says the last shall be first, and the first shall be last. God is creating and doing a new thing in God's people. Please know that God will never forget His people, and God's love is everlasting. God is a way maker, a promise keeper, and the light in the darkness.

If you want or need change, only God can do it. God did it for me.

1
THE CALL

I am Latonya Morrison. I was born on August 1, 1980, the eighth month of the year and the first day of the month. In my immediate family, I am the first to have a son. My son was also his father's first child and only son. I was the first black girl to work behind the counter as a cashier in an all-white business. I gave my life to Christ at the age of 18 years old. I became the first minister of the Gospel in my family, born in the 80s generation.

At that time, I didn't know God for who He is today. I used to sing at different churches, which made me want to know who God was. As I got older and started to experience this nation called America, I began to regret who God was and who He started showing me who He was. As I went on, while I was still living a worldly life and not thinking about the life I had already given to God, things in this nation started turning against me. I thought God had forgotten about me just as I had indeed forgotten about God. Thankfully, God sent a longtime friend to bring me back to church. As I went to this church, the pastor always preached a good word, but there was no connection. I thought that if I had joined the church, maybe I would have felt a connection, but it didn't work out. I stopped going.

I was lost and did not understand why life was so hard. I used to ask myself, where did you go wrong? I had great, bad, and some days when I did not want to be here. Then I figured enough is enough, and I surrendered to God!

There was a point after surrendering to God: I wanted to hear from God and to hear His voice again. So, back in 2013, my life went astray even after surrendering. I didn't know what to do. I was so angry, hurt, and mentally all over the place. I even got arrested, and it made me feel like I was never going to amount to anything. But God sent my best friend, and we went to her auntie's church. Her auntie began to prophesize to me. At the time, I did not know what that meant. I was afraid to allow her to touch me until she said God said, "Don't be afraid." I returned home, knelt, and said, "Lord, please lead me and guide me so I can live a better life and start hearing from you."

Oh, and did God answer my prayers? Yes, He did because I kept attending church to learn and build my relationship with God. Then boom, I started hearing and writing for God. Some read my writing and didn't truly believe God was speaking through me that way. As people began to read what God gave me, the more they thought it wasn't true. I started to doubt myself until God spoke these words to me.

God said, "Don't worry. They will read and listen someday because the things I speak to you about are what I need you to do for me. I need you to let my people know this is the time for your faith to be tested. The United States of America needs to come together in unity. All those who believe in me need to unite and save those who do not believe in me."

Reflection Time

Have you ever had challenges that made you doubt God was with you? How did you overcome these challenges?

2
A DIVINE CALL FOR ALL AMERICANS

And God said to me,

All the hope, grace, and mercy with the American people is not being used.

They have a standard that I don't care about; their hearts are not pure; they idolize things that are not as important as Me.

Americans do not realize how much pain they are putting Me through. I am loving, caring, graceful, merciful, and forgiving. The American people realize nothing but greed, the power that is not powerful. Do they not know that I will destroy everything they created if they do not worship Me?

The world can think that I don't exist. The American people need to get their act together. Not worshipping Me, the creator of all things, means you do not believe in Me. When good things happen to rich Americans, they fail because they sell their souls! I am losing my people, and that's because those who say they have faith in Me are strong yet afraid to step out on faith and compel others to come to Christ.

Anyone in human flesh who worships and believes in I Am, God the Father, can step out on faith with permission to do

3

anything you have to believe. That's why I (God) can take certain people to complete specific tasks. I need the United States of America to see and know this.

Reflection Time

Think about this message.

How does this make you look at your own life and your choices?

Are there ways to start living closer to what God wants, even if it means going against what everyone else is doing or what you're afraid of?

3
MY CHILDREN

To my fellow children that love Me dearly,

Take a stand and take your nation back. I give you the real power to stand against the enemy. Use it! Don't be afraid to speak your mind and make powerful moves. If I Am for you, who in this world can be against you? Come together. All united and be as one. You are all serving Me. Even though most of my preachers have their own place to worship, I Am God.

I still need all of my saints to come together. All saints come together and fight. Use the anointed power. I will order your steps. Listen, listen, listen. Please, my saints, you don't know how much power you can accomplish together as a whole.

The devil will flee.

Be bold.

Be courageous.

Be mighty.

And keep strong faith!

Your American nation can win if you read this book, apply what I am saying, and use it to your advantage.

Stop being weak.

This is just the beginning of the test, and this is a warning to let my saints know you all have to come and unite. Unity, unity, unity, saints!

I Am God is going to show the American nation who is in charge.

Reflection Time

Take this advice to be brave, stand up for your beliefs, and keep a strong faith in your everyday life. God is with you. Be bold!

4
BUILT ARMY

Step in and use the real power. Please don't be afraid because I will be with you.

My servants, you must stay focused. Praying and fasting will help you build your faith and hear from me. Take heed to what I am saying. We need more revivals and deliverance services.

Work on building up your families so that it will be easier for my people to fight. It's time to put everything else aside. Focus on I Am so the army I am building will learn to fight well so my people can be set free in this nation.

I need you to understand that this book is of my word. I am speaking directly to my servant, and she is telling the world.

It is now time to fight for the American nation! I have watched so much of my American nation be unappreciative! They destroyed everything. The American people never took the time to ask what I wanted America to be. They just took me out of the equation. They think they're so powerful, but they are powerless.

So, I want my army. You know who you are. Get ready to fight this battle! Serve, rejoice, pray, and fast so you can receive the power of Me and not of this world.

The army that I Am God is creating is those who can defeat the greedy and powerful people in the United States of America. If you do not get on one accord and let my people go, you will feel the wrath of Me. You will no longer keep them bound as you have.

Unity is all that my people want and need. This time has come for you to understand that when I give you power, you are not to be against one another. You are to work together and build the nation that I have put you in control of, not to break people who are loving and caring human beings. I didn't put my people on earth to do these things!

It's not a white-and-black issue; it is spiritual. I Am God, and I can do all things. I give the American nation so much grace and mercy. I Am God. I can change every living being in the United States of America to be one color or not to have any color at all. Then what will the American people do?

This battle is spiritual. America has to get itself together. For you, American human beings, know that you will feel the spirit of I Am God when you read this. I Am God. This is my warning to you because it seems that no one is listening.

Reflection Time

Are you listening for God's voice to give you direction for your life? Seek God and hear His voice.

5
BELIEVE

To my people who serve, I am God. Don't quit. Believe in me. Believe like you have never believed before. Those who are last will be first. I am God Jehovah Jireh speaking to you, so take this word and keep it in your heart. Do not let the words you read in the book or Bible be misunderstood. Love those I have given you.

Love is the power. Love is power. Forgive those who hurt you. Let all the pasts go and move forward within. I am God. Stay humble, and do not act like you are better.

Humble is the way. Be bold and only speak the words to all who read this book. I will speak to you only if you believe the words that I say in this book. Stand firm on who you believe in.

My people do not be afraid to stand on what you believe. Do not be afraid to use the power I have given each of you! Hear, hear, hear, hear. It is the Lord Almighty. We are in a time now where you must use your faith. Use it, use it, use it. I will stand with you in these times of battle. America has allowed the enemy to declare war on all human life!

America will go through some very hard times. The world is so lost and distant. All my people live in the same place, earth, yet so distant. All were born into the world with one mind: the brain and one heart that all look the same. The only thing that makes mankind's life different is what the heart and mind intake.

They listen and focus on things that are not important. Because the things they allow the mind to intake are not of, I am God. Do things I set in your heart. But humankind fears the feeling of the heart. They allow the mind to tell the heart what to do instead of the heart telling the mind. You must have a clear mind and allow God to fill your heart so the mind can intake what your heart feels.

The only way to clear the mind is to have faith and trust that I Am God will lead you and guide you through all things. This is a message to the entire United States of America. You must bring me back to this nation, or you shall fail.

To all my believers, go and save my people. You know the way! Now is the time to go. No judgment. No hard feelings. Go and save my people who don't know my name or who I AM. You have the power. America needs help desperately. Do what I have called my people to do. God save this nation. God save this nation! I will not give up on my people that worship I AM God. Take heed to what I say and whom I speak through because I have no respect of persons.

I Am God will take a nobody as the world would see them and make them into someone. All I ask of my people is not to deny me. As well as living, I need my people to:

1. Put off your old self.
2. Put on your New Self – put on the armor of God
3. Put off the flash hood – not to be arrogant.
4. Speak truthfully to your neighbor.
5. In anger, do not sin.
6. Do not let the sun go down while still angry.

7. Do not give the devil a foothold.
8. No stealing.
9. Do not let any unwholesome talk come out of your mouth.
10. Do not grieve the Holy Spirit of God.
11. Get rid of all bitterness, rage, anger, brawling, and slander, along with every form of malice.
12. Be kind and compassionate to one another, forgiving each other just as God forgave you.
13. There must not be even a hint of sexual immorality.
14. Or any kind of impurity or greed
15. Nor should there be obscenity, foolish talk, or coarse joking which are out of place but instead thanksgiving, no immoral, impure, or greedy person – an idolater.
16. Let no one deceive you.
17. Having nothing to do with fruitless deeds of darkness. Expose them.
18. Do not get drunk on wine.

Reflection Time

Do you believe God wants the best for your life? Are you willing to follow His principles to achieve this?

6
WHO IS JESUS?

Jesus is the Bread of Life

John 6:35

Jesus is the Living Water

John 7:38

Jesus is the Light of the World.

John 8:12

Reflection Time

Which description of Jesus resonates with you the most? Why?

PRAISE

Believe in me as you believe in yourself.

Don't be afraid to clap, dance, lift hands, praise, and sing!

7
I AM

I AM that I AM.

I AM the bread of life.

John 6:35: "And Jesus said unto them, I am the bread of life: he that cometh to me shall never hunger; and he that believeth on me shall never thirst."

John 6:48: "I am that bread of life."

I AM the light of the world.

John 8:12: "Then spake Jesus again unto them, saying, I am the light of the world: he that followeth me shall not walk in darkness, but shall have the light of life."

John 9:5: "As long as I am in the world, I am the light of the world."

I AM the door.

John 10:7: "Then said Jesus unto them again, Verily, verily, I say unto you, I am the door of the sheep."

John 10:9: "I am the door: by me if any man enter in, he shall be saved, and shall go in and out, and find pasture."

I AM the good shepherd.

John 10:11: "I am the good shepherd: the good shepherd giveth his life for the sheep."

John 10:14: "I am the good shepherd, and know my sheep, and am known of mine."

I AM the resurrection and the life.

John 11:25: "Jesus said unto her, I am the resurrection, and the life: he that believeth in me, though he were dead, yet shall he live:"

I AM the way, the truth, and the life.

John 14:6: "Jesus saith unto him, I am the way, the truth, and the life: no man cometh unto the Father, but by me."

I AM the true vine.

John 15:1: "I am the true vine, and my Father is the husbandman."

John 15:5: "I am the vine, ye are the branches: He that abideth in me, and I in him, the same bringeth forth much fruit: for without me ye can do nothing."

"I AM" is the one who allows the animals to roam free, as my people should the winds blow only because of me.

"I AM" is love. Love is what and who we are! The United States means nothing without "I AM."

My fellow people, enjoy the things I have given you. The wind, rain, trees, sand, water, heat, clouds, and stars. These are the beautiful things in life that human beings don't enjoy.

Reflection Time

What does "I AM" mean to you? What is the significance of "I AM" in your life?

8
DON'T BE A COMPLAINER

When you appreciate things, there is no room to complain! See, we as people are the opposite. We complain about everything and barely appreciate anything.

God wants us to appreciate everything because God allows everything that goes on in our lives to happen. So, if we complain about the things in our lives, that is a slap in God's face because He is the beginning and the end! God created the story of our lives, and He ends it. I was a complainer like the Israelites, and Moses and Aaron helped flee from Egypt. I was always complaining about this about that. One of my biggest complaints was, "Why am I always alone?"

It wasn't until I built my relationship with God that He said to appreciate being alone so you can learn your worth. Once you learn your worth, it is easier not to settle for anything. Another complaint was, "Why wasn't my dad in my life?" God said to appreciate that he wasn't there. He would have blocked your strength.

Another complaint I had was, "Why did my mom never show me love?" God said because I wouldn't have learned to love myself. Looking back over my life, I have learned to appreciate the good and the bad. We, as people, can be so busy complaining about the bad that we don't realize the bad is good. Because if it wasn't for the bad, we couldn't appreciate the goodness of the Lord. Bad is an experience, and good is growth.

Reflection Time

What are two things that you appreciate in your life at this moment?

9
RIDING WITH THE MAN
WHO HAS THE PLAN

To know God's plan for your life, you have got to get out of your way! We paralyze ourselves, thinking that we cannot move forward. We have to want change for things to be different. Change is something that I wanted and still want. Therefore, I have to move out of the driver's seat and allow God to drive with Jesus on the other side while I'm in the back!

With fear, doubt, procrastination, and disbelief in the trunk with the rest of the junk that keeps me in the way of God's plan for my life. We have to move out of the way. Let go and let God! What's the purpose of God having a plan for your life if you can't live out the plan? Move and allow God to take the wheel and drive. I promise it will be a smooth ride because Jesus is on the other side.

Reflection Time

What "wheel" are you holding on to that's prohibiting God from driving? Are you ready to release it?

USE YOUR POWER

To my fellow believers, go and save the United States of America. Use your power.

10
WHAT DOES GOD MEAN TO YOU?

In the Bible, many scriptures tell us how God feels about mankind! I Corinthians 10:13 says, "No temptation has overtaken you except what is common to mankind. And God is faithful; He will not let you be tempted beyond what you can bear. But when you are tempted, he will also provide a way out so that you can endure it." I John 1:5 states, "this message we heard from him and declare to you: God is light in Him there is no darkness at all."

We also have other Bible scriptures where God always tells us how much we mean to him. In 2 Peter 3:9, Genesis 1:1, Hebrews 4:12, James 1 17, and more, God tells us how much He loves us. So now the question is, what does God mean to you?

God wants to know. If He didn't tell you that He would bless you, would you still worship Him? If I didn't send my son Jesus Christ to die on the cross for your sins, would you still love me? Whenever you prayed and I didn't answer, would you still love me? If I only give mankind life with no instruction, would you still love me? Some of God's people only love and do things for one another because they may have done something for them. But what about those that do nothing for you? Can we love them the same? We should because God does multiple things for us. And half of God's people come to the house of the Lord and do not worship Him or praise Him! As much as God does for mankind, why are we so afraid to show the meaning and love we have for Him anywhere and anytime?

God said if I am for you, who in this world can be against you. Romans 8:31 - Therefore, if God can bless us in front of everyone around us and people who don't even know us, why can't we do the same for Him? People who don't even know you can see the love of God when you do because of the light he shines on you! No one in this world can give you the light of God. God wants to know how much He means to us. Do you love me more than the material things I bless you with? Do you love me more than the people I have given you to love? Do you love and trust me more than the air you breathe? Do you believe in what was created by men more than me?

As mankind, are we still loving those who don't believe in God? Are we helping those who can't help themselves, regardless of circumstances? If we are doing those things, that is showing God how much He means to us.

Are we still loving our neighbor as we love ourselves? If people ask, tell them that we love you with the love of God. Are we praising God through the good and bad? Are we helping one another clean the specks from each other's eyes?

Are we blessing others because God blesses us? If we do those things, we allow God to see what He means to us! God bless everyone because God is love!

Reflection Time

What does God mean to you?

11
INVITE GOD INTO YOUR SPACE

God is…

The one who will never tell your secrets.

The one you call on, and He answers when He is invited.

The one who makes your dark day turn into sunshine.

The one who can make a way out of no way.

The one when times get hard, God will let you know it's going to be okay.

The one who forgives you no matter what.

The one that will always love you unconditionally.

The one who has the power to heal when sickness comes.

The one who sees more in you than you would ever see in yourself.

The one who can make your enemy your footstool and will fight all your battles only if you cast your cares on Him, for He cares for us.

The one who gave His only son for our sins.

Who wouldn't invite a friend like God! God wants to be invited. Invite God into your life so He can be the best and closest friend you will ever have.

Reflection Time

Have you invited God into your life? If yes, how has God changed your life?

What holds you back if you have not invited God into your life?

12
GOD IS WORKING BEHIND THE SCENES

Trust in the Lord with all your heart, and do not lean on your own understanding. Proverbs 3:5

No matter what is going on in your life, you must trust God.

Example: What comes to mind when you think of a famous movie? It could be your favorite actor or actress. Or could it be the way the film was created? I know everyone wondered how they make movies seem so real and interesting. It's the people who work behind the scenes. The director, producer, casting director, and the visual effects. These are some of the people who work behind the scenes to make a great movie.

See, to make a movie, we need all types of people, but in our lives, we have God working behind the scenes for us. When we think God is not with us, He's behind the scenes. When we think God's not listening, He's listening behind the scenes. God works behind the scenes for us. God is our director, producer, casting director, and more to ensure our lives are the greatest we can ever see. So don't give up on God when you cannot trace

Him. Just know God is working behind the scenes of your life. God will never leave you nor forsake you.

God will create a life so great everyone will know who's working behind the scenes.

Reflection Time

What are you trusting God to work on "behind the scenes" in your life? Write one scripture that aligns with it.

13
BECOME A LABOURER

The harvest truly is plenteous, but the labourers are few. Matthew 9:37

Labourer- A person doing unskilled manual work for wages.

We, the people, are doing too much for mankind. God is our creator, not man. There are few labourers because most people choose to serve man before God. Exodus 34:14 says, Do not worship any other God for the Lord, whose name is Jealous, is a jealous God. If you are doing so much for man, when do you decide to find and focus on your Godly purpose? To be a labourer of God, you must know your purpose. "For many are called but few are chosen." Matthew 22:14

To be chosen not only means to be favored, but it also requires responsible actions. God said you are chosen now to have strong faith and the power to seek the ones called for labourers. If the chosen, even those with titles, would humble themselves and become labourers, we can get those who need to be saved.

God says to stop focusing so much on man's work. Do the work that I have called you to do. Go out and get the ones called but don't know their purpose for the Lord. If God has chosen you, you must know He has given you the power to do the work.

Reflection Time

Are you willing to be a labourer for Christ? Take a moment to think about this. How can you help bring others to Christ?

ABOUT THE AUTHOR

LaTonya Sherron Morrison, a trailblazer from Raeford, NC, is the first in her generation to embrace ministry, navigating life's hurdles with unwavering faith. Born to Annie Pearl Morrison, Latonya's roots run deep in her close-knit community. Her transformative journey took her from aspirations in beauty to profound spiritual awakening at 35, dedicating her life to Jesus Christ and spreading the Gospel and personal growth development through cooking, reading, and writing.

Today, she embarks on her latest calling: sharing divine inspirations through her debut book which is a testament to God's love and power to reshape lives.

Made in the USA
Columbia, SC
01 October 2024